Prime Ministers of Canada

Time of Turmoil

By Douglas Baldwin and Patricia Baldwin

Weigl

CALGARY
www.weigl.com

Published by Weigl Educational Publishers Limited
6325 10 Street SE
Calgary, Alberta, Canada
T2H 2Z9

Website: www.weigl.com

Library and Archives Canada Cataloguing in Publication

Rossiter, Mary Juanita
     Contemporary Canada / Mary Juanita Rossiter.
(Prime ministers of Canada)
Includes index.
ISBN 1-55388-256-3 (bound).--ISBN 1-55388-247-4 (pbk.)
     1. Prime ministers--Canada--Biography--Textbooks.
2. Canada--History--1963- --Textbooks. I. Title. II. Series:
Prime ministers of Canada (Calgary, Alta.)
FC26.P7R68 2006   971.064'70922   C2006-902488-X

Printed in Canada
1 2 3 4 5 6 7 8 9 0 10 09 08 07 06

Cover: William Lyon Mackenzie King was Canada's longest-serving prime minister.

Photo Credits: Glenbow Museum Archives: pages 5 (nc-6-11899), 34 (nc-6-11899), 38 (nc-6-12955b), 39 (NA-2903-55); **Library and Archives Canada:** pages 4 (C-005327, C-010460, PA-033933, C-001971), 5 (C-00687, PA-128175), 20, 26 (C-022001), 27 (PA-128229), 29 (C-024452), 36 (C-00687); **Saskatchewan Archives:** page 4 (R-D700).

We acknowledge the financial support of the Government of Canada through the Book Publishing Program (BPIDP) for our publishing activities.

Project Coordinator
Tatiana Tomljanovic

Design
Terry Paulhus

Contents

Canada's Prime Ministers 4

William Lyon Mackenzie King: Canada's
Longest-Serving Prime Minister 6

King's Early Years 8

Special People in King's Life 10

Becoming Prime Minister 12

The Man Behind the Politician 14

King Enters the Spirit World 16

King and Canadian Independence . .18

Women in Parliament 20

The "King-Byng Wing Ding" 21

King and Dictators 22

King and World War II 24

French-Canadians
and Conscription 26

King and War-Time Pressures 28

King's Diaries 30

King and the United States 31

King's Final Years 32

Arthur Meighen 34

Richard Bedford Bennett 36

Bennett and the Great Depression . .38

Timeline 40

Did You Know? 42

Test Your Knowledge 43

Activity .44

Further Research 45

Glossary .46

Political Terms 47

Index 48

Canada's Prime Ministers

Since **Confederation**, there have been 22 Canadian prime ministers. Canada's prime ministers have come from many provinces and cultures. Some of them, such as the first prime minister, John A. Macdonald, were born in other countries. They came to Canada because they, or their parents, decided Canada was the best place to live and raise a family.

Canada's prime ministers are people of many talents and different interests. Some trained as lawyers, while others were journalists, doctors, farmers, writers, teachers, business people, and members of the **civil service**. Some of them fought as soldiers to protect Canada and her allies. All of them had one thing in common. They wanted to make Canada one of the best places in the world to live.

THE NEW NATION (CONFEDERATION TO 1896)

 John A. Macdonald
(July 1, 1867–November 5, 1873; October 17,1878–June 6, 1891)

 Alexander Mackenzie
(November 7, 1873–October 8, 1878)

 John J. C. Abbott
(June 16, 1891–November 24, 1892)

 John S. D. Thompson
(December 5, 1892–December 12, 1894)

 Mackenzie Bowell
(December 21, 1894–April 27, 1896)

 Charles H. Tupper
(May 1, 1896–July 8, 1896)

TURN OF THE 20ᵀᴴ CENTURY (1896–1920)

 Wilfrid Laurier
(July 11, 1896–October 6, 1911)

 Robert L. Borden
(October 10, 1911–July 10, 1920)

TIME OF TURMOIL (1920–1948)

 Arthur Meighen
(July 10, 1920–December 29,1921;
June 29, 1926–
September 25, 1926)

 Richard B. Bennett
(August 7, 1930–
October 23, 1935)

**William Lyon Mackenzie
King**(December 29, 1921–June 28,
1926; September 25, 1926–August
7, 1930; October 23, 1935–
November 15, 1948)

TIME OF TRANSITION (1948–1968)

 Louis S. Saint Laurent
(November 15, 1948–
June 21, 1957)

 John George Diefenbaker
(June 21, 1957–
April 22, 1963)

 Lester B. Pearson
(April 22, 1963–
April 20, 1968)

TRUDEAU ERA (1968–1984)

 Pierre Elliott Trudeau
(April 20, 1968–June 3,
1979; March 3, 1980–
June 30, 1984)

 Charles Joseph Clark
(June 4, 1979–
March 2, 1980)

John N. Turner
(June 30, 1984–
September 17, 1984)

CONTEMPORARY CANADA (1984 TO PRESENT)

 Martin Brian Mulroney
(September 17, 1984–
June 13, 1993)

Jean J. Chrétien
(October 25, 1993–
December 12, 2003)

Kim Campbell
(June 13, 1993–
October 25, 1993)

 Paul E. P. Martin
(December 12, 2003–
February 6, 2006)

 Stephen J. Harper
(February 6, 2006–)

William Lyon Mackenzie King: Canada's Longest-Serving Prime Minister

Prime Minister King did more than any prime minister before him to gain Canadian independence from Great Britain.

As a teenager, William Lyon Mackenzie King wrote in his diary, "Surely I have some great work to accomplish before I die." King served more years as prime minister than any other Canadian. He led Canada through the 1920s, part of the **Great Depression** of the 1930s, and World War II. His decisions during these times of turmoil shaped Canada and its position in the world.

In 1997, several experts, including historians, were asked to rank Canada's prime ministers on a scale from 0 to 10. Fourteen of the historians ranked King as Canada's "greatest" prime minister. While they did not like King as a person, they admired his devotion to Canadian unity. They liked the way he brought Canada through World War II, helped create the British Commonwealth, and began Canada's social welfare policies for the less fortunate.

"It is what we prevent, rather than what we do that counts most in government." This statement sums up King's political career. He did not have an exciting image. He did not give spellbinding speeches, and he supported few radical policies. Yet, King is considered by some to be Canada's most effective prime minister.

King was prime minister of Canada for 22 years.

Keeping Canada Together

"I have been able to serve my country in the government, to keep an honest and just administration... It is all with a spirit of humble gratitude that I thank God for it all."
William Lyon Mackenzie King

King's Early Years

> "Dear Father, to be like him in spirit and in heart is my ambition now... It has been a joy to reflect... that he and mother and I dined together here, that we shared music and song together and sweet companionship... How sacred these remembrances are now."
>
> *An excerpt from King's diary, written shortly after his father's death in 1916*

King's mother, Isabel Mackenzie, was the daughter of William Lyon Mackenzie. She had been born in the United States while her father was in exile for leading the 1837 **rebellion** in **Upper Canada**. In 1849, the government allowed William Lyon Mackenzie to return to Canada. He did so the following year.

John King was born shortly after the death of his father, an officer in the army that fought against Mackenzie in the 1837 rebellion. John was raised by his widowed mother and her brother. He became a lawyer in Berlin, Ontario. In 1872, he married Isabel Mackenzie. The couple settled in Berlin.

William Lyon Mackenzie King was born on December 17, 1874. He was the eldest of four children. King spent his early childhood in Woodside, where the family lived for seven years.

"Willie," as his family called him, grew up in a loving family. He was a busy, active boy. Willie took piano and dance classes, played sports, and went camping. At school, Willie was a good student. He joined a debating club and became interested in politics.

Isabel spent many hours telling her eldest son about his grandfather, William Lyon Mackenzie. His grandfather, she said, was the hero of the 1837 rebellion because he fought for democracy and for the common man. King grew up wanting to serve his country, just like his grandfather had done.

In 1891, King went to the University of Toronto to study political science. He was a hard worker, had a good memory, and was well organized. He graduated second in his class.

At university, King remained active. He played sports, wrote for the university newspaper, and attended church regularly. He also visited patients in the hospital and helped the less fortunate. Respected

King's grandfather, William Lyon Mackenzie, was born in Scotland. In 1837, he led an unsuccessful rebellion against the ruling class in Upper Canada.

by his classmates, King was elected president of his freshman class. It was at this time that he began to sign his name as "W. L. King." His family still called him Willie, but his friends referred to him as Mackenzie.

As a student, King became interested in **labour unions**. At Harvard University in 1898, he researched the problems of workers in the clothing industry. He even wrote to the government to complain about the poor treatment of workers.

In 1900, King accepted a job as deputy minister in the Department of Labour. He wrote that it provided him with a chance to continue his grandfather's example of public service. In 1908, he was elected to **Parliament**. Liberal Prime Minister Wilfrid Laurier later appointed King minister of labour. Three years later, the Liberals lost the 1911 election. King moved to the United States in 1914, where he worked as a labour consultant for the Rockefeller Foundation. He took the job on the condition that he could return to Canada when another election was called.

At Harvard University, King became interested in the politics of labour. He sympathized with workers in the clothing industry, whom he felt were treated very poorly.

Special People in King's Life

Other than his mother and siblings, King was not close to many people. He spent most of his time with other politicians, such as U.S. President Franklin Roosevelt and British Prime Minister Winston Churchill.

Isabel, King's mother, was probably the most important person in King's life. He adored her. "Anything more lovely than her face and presence I have never known," he wrote in his diary. Isabel was warm and outgoing. She visited King often. "She is, I think, the purest and sweetest soul that God ever made. She is all tenderness and love, all devotion, knows nothing of selfishness and thinks only of others."

After the deaths of her daughter Bella in 1915 and her husband John in 1916, Isabel spent most of her time with her eldest son. In 1917, she suffered a stroke. Her health steadily declined. When Isabel passed away later that year, King felt painfully alone.

King called his oldest sister "Bella." In 1898, Bella went to Boston to study nursing. She enjoyed the work, but her father and brother Willie disapproved. King saw Bella often while she was in Boston. In his diary, he frequently mentioned Bella and his belief that nursing was not the right job for her. "I think Bella will likely go home by Xmas. At least I will seek so to persuade her." Bella returned home. She never married and spent much of her time caring for her aging parents, doing church work, and working with young people. King's diary contains many affectionate references to Bella.

"Jennie," King's sister, was the most fun-loving member of the King family. In letters to King, she stated that she was very proud of him. In 1893, the family moved to Toronto. Jennie spent much of her time teaching street children and running a girls' club.

In 1906, Jennie married Harry Morrison Lay, a long time friend of the Kings. Harry Lay passed away in 1945, and Jennie died in 1962.

"Max," King's brother, was the youngest member of the family. After a sickly childhood, he studied medicine and became a doctor. In 1902, he went to South Africa to spend time with a medical corps during the Boer War. He returned to Canada, settled in Ottawa, and established his own medical practice.

Max married Mae Wookey in 1911. They had twin sons. Shortly after the birth of his boys, Max contracted tuberculosis. Before Max died, King visited him. He wrote in his diary, "It has been a terrible business, but he has set a noble and brave example…. I shall miss Max greatly. For 8 years we have corresponded every week and he has been constantly in my thoughts. He was the only one left who is really interested in my life and work." When Max died, King lost not only a brother but a friend on whom he could count for honest advice.

King wrote about the details of his life and his family in his journals for 58 years.

Becoming Prime Minister

> "When I was chosen leader of the party it was said by my opponents, and by some others, that I would not last long in that position."
>
> *King*

One of King's most important decisions came before he ran for prime minister during the 1917 election. The issue was **conscription**. Most French-Canadians, including Liberal Party leader Wilfrid Laurier, did not think that Canadians should be forced to fight in World War I. Many English-speaking Canadians wanted to force people to fight. King decided to support Laurier. Although Laurier lost the 1917 election, French-Canadians remembered that King had stood by Laurier. When Laurier died in 1919, King was elected as the Liberal Party leader.

King could not speak French. To ensure that he did not ignore the French-Canadian point of view, he worked closely with a French-Canadian. Ernest Lapointe filled this role until his death in 1941. Louis St. Laurent took Lapointe's place and became prime minister when King resigned in 1948.

In 1921, Arthur Meighen, the prime minister and Conservative Party leader, called an election. The voters blamed Meighen for the high cost of living. French-Canadians blamed him for conscription. As a result, only 50 Conservatives were elected. William Lyon King was now the prime minister of Canada. He wrote that his victory justified his grandfather's "great purpose and aim."

After the defeat of Laurier's government in 1911, King went to work in the United States, but returned to Canada in 1917 to fight alongside Laurier in the national election.

LIBERAL PARTY CONVENTION

Until the Liberal convention of 1919, party leaders were chosen behind closed doors by the party's senators and members of Parliament. King was the first political party leader to be elected by the members of his party.

In April 1930, the Conservatives argued that the growth of **unemployment** during the Great Depression was so serious that Ottawa should provide financial help to the provinces. The provincial governments were responsible for unemployment relief. King did not want to provide additional funding to the provinces. He pointed out that no premier had asked for assistance and said that he would not give a provincial Conservative government "a five-cent piece." In the federal election that July, this "five-cent speech" cost him the victory. Even so, the severity of the Great Depression of the 1930s would have defeated any government. Conservative Party leader Richard Bedford Bennett replaced King as prime minister. However, as the Depression worsened, Bennett was blamed by Canadians for the poor economy. As a result, King returned to power in 1935. He remained prime minister until 1948.

The second man to work as Prime Minister King's advisor on French-Canadian issues was Louis St. Laurent, a future prime minister.

BERLIN BECOMES KITCHENER

The town of Berlin had been settled by German immigrants. By the beginning of World War I, Berlin had several German-language societies. Since Germany was Canada's enemy in the war, some people distrusted Canadians of German descent. In 1914, a bronze statue of German leader Kaiser Wilhelm that stood in the town park was thrown into the lake. The Berlin Board of Trade recommended that the city change its name to show that the town supported Canada's soldiers. On September 1, 1916, the citizens voted to change the town's name to Kitchener. Horatio Kitchener had been the British Secretary for War.

The Man Behind the Politician

> "Dear little soul, he is almost human. I sometimes think he is a comforter dear mother has sent to me, he is filled with her spirit of patience, and tenderness and love."
>
> *An excerpt from King's diary about his dog Pat*

King had few interests outside of politics. He sometimes had guests for dinner, but this usually only took place on formal occasions. He was not friends with any of his fellow party members, and was not close to his only remaining family, his sister Jennie. Many who knew King remembered him as a very lonely man. Newspaper reporter Bruce Hutchison once called him "the loneliest man in Canada."

King's closest friend was Joan Patteson. She was the wife of a local banker. Patteson was a sympathetic woman and a good listener. She made no demands on King's time and often helped him entertain. They talked regularly. Patteson and her husband Godfrey were both friends with King. He was a frequent dinner guest in the Patteson's home. King came to depend on them, especially Joan, for companionship and moral support. They went on long walks together, often with their dogs. Patteson shared King's interest in the **spirit** world as well.

King and his beloved dog, Pat, enjoyed many morning walks together.

In July 1924, the Pattesons gave King an Irish terrier. He named the dog Pat and became extremely fond of the animal. King mentioned Pat in his diary almost every day for the next 17 years. He was King's closest companion. They often went for morning walks and shared evening snacks of oatmeal cookies and Ovaltine. Pat died in 1941. King wrote in his diary at the end of the year, "As I think it all over tonight, the event that touched me most deeply of all was perhaps the death of little Pat... That little dog has taught me how to live, and also how to look forward, without concern, to the arms that will be around me when I, too, pass away. We shall all be together in the Beyond. Of that I am perfectly sure."

Two other Pats followed. Pat II died in 1947 of cancer. He was to undergo surgery, but the disease was too far advanced, and he was put to sleep to spare him further pain. Of Pat II, King wrote, "Little Pat lay on the bed and was very friendly. He is becoming a dear dog." After King's death in 1950, Pat III was given to friends.

After Pat's death, King kept a memorial picture of the dog on his mantle.

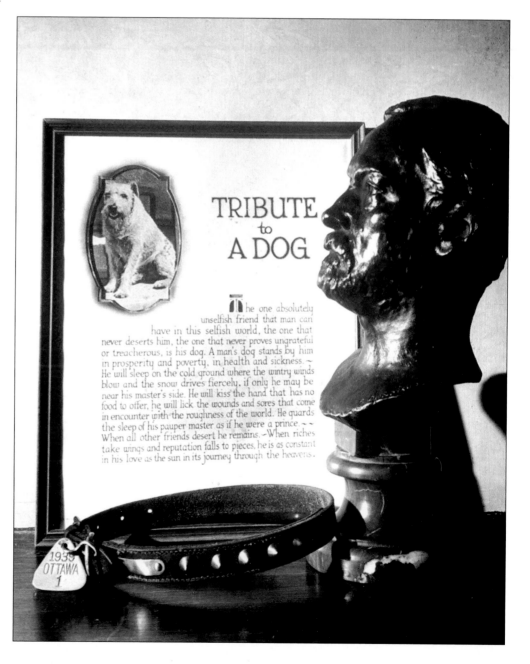

TRIBUTE
to
A DOG

The one absolutely unselfish friend that man can have in this selfish world, the one that never deserts him, the one that never proves ungrateful or treacherous, is his dog. A man's dog stands by him in prosperity and poverty, in health and sickness. ~ He will sleep on the cold ground where the wintry winds blow and the snow drives fiercely, if only he may be near his master's side. He will kiss the hand that has no food to offer, he will lick the wounds and sores that come in encounter with the roughness of the world. He guards the sleep of his pauper master as if he were a prince. ~ ~ When all other friends desert he remains. ~ When riches take wings and reputation falls to pieces, he is as constant in his love as the sun in its journey through the heavens.

King Enters the Spirit World

> "The 'conversations' in many cases have been so loud, so clear etc. that I have felt great embarrassment at the servants in other parts of the house, hearing what was said, as I am sure they have."
>
> *An excerpt from King's diary excerpt on talking to the dead*

After King's death, many Canadians were surprised to learn that the former prime minister was interested in the spirit world.

At first, King was doubtful about spiritualism. However, following the loss of four members of his family in seven years, he became lonely. It was partly out of this loneliness that he tried speaking to his dead relatives.

King had consulted a fortuneteller, Rachel Bleaney, in 1896. She correctly predicted that he would travel to Chicago in the fall. In 1925, Bleaney claimed that she saw the spirits of King's mother and brother Max. In another reading, she correctly predicted that King would win the 1926 election after a hard fight. However, he was somewhat disillusioned when he lost the election of 1930 after Bleaney suggested that he would win.

In 1932, King met Etta Wriedt. Wriedt was a "direct voice" **medium** who used a small, folding, trumpet-shaped instrument to

King was very interested in spiritualism and made frequent attempts to speak to the spirits of loved ones who had passed away.

King was very superstitious. He checked the hands of the clock whenever something significant occurred. If they were together, opposite, or at right angles, he believed that someone in the "other world" was watching over him.

communicate with the dead. At several **séances**, King believed he had talked with his dead mother, father, grandfather, brother, sisters, and Wilfrid Laurier. He wrote, "There can be no doubt whatsoever that the persons I have been talking with were the loved ones and others I have known and who have passed away. It was the spirits of the departed."

King believed that dreams were another method of communicating with the dead. He recorded his dreams so that he could interpret them later. By the 1940s, he felt that dreams were the most reliable means of contacting the spirit world.

King's involvement in spiritualism did not affect his actions as prime minister. The messages tended to confirm his ideas, warned him to proceed cautiously, and encouraged him to be true to his ideals. Spiritualism provided King with comfort and support. He believed that his family members, friends, and former colleagues were still with him, guiding him and giving him their approval.

DID YOU KNOW?

King was interested in tea leaf readings. Some people believe that a person's fortune or future can be revealed by the pattern of tea leaves left in a cup after drinking the tea.

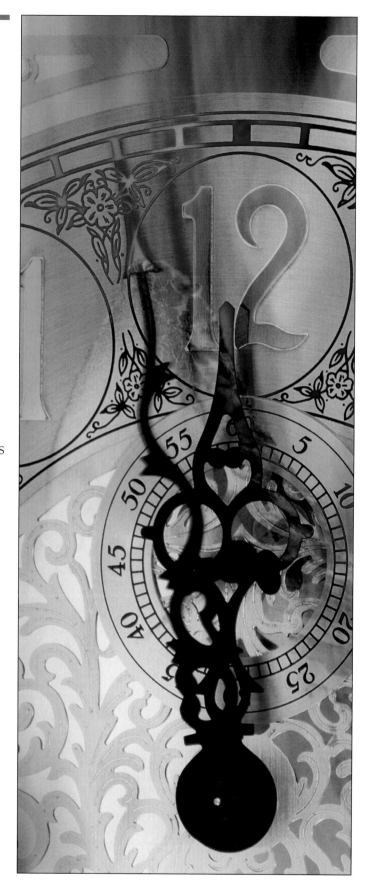

King and Canadian Independence

> "His Excellency [the governor general] spoke of the Treaty, said it had given him pleasure to see it accomplished....I told His Excellency I was sure it was right to remove any badge of 'colonialism'."
>
> *King on Canada signing the Halibut Treaty independently of Great Britain*

DARDANELLES STRAIT

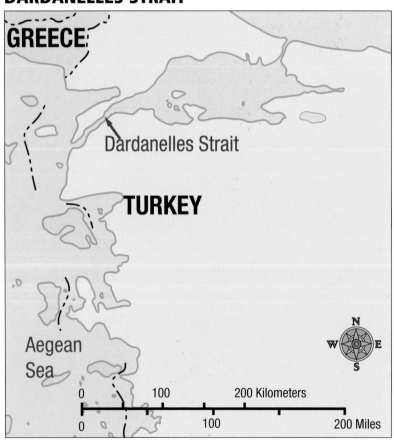

When King became prime minister, Great Britain controlled Canada's relations with other countries. Canada was still a British **colony**. King helped create the British Commonwealth. He was also responsible for Canada becoming independent of Great Britain.

The Chanak Crisis of 1922 was the first step in this direction. In September, Turkey threatened to occupy the area of Chanak on the Dardanelles strait. Great Britain wanted to prevent the occupation. They asked Canada to send troops. Instead of agreeing, as Canadian prime ministers were expected to do, King refused to send troops. He said that the Canadian Parliament would have to decide. Arthur Meighen, the Conservative leader, disagreed. He said that Canada should reply, "Ready, aye ready; we stand by you," and send troops in support. When Turkey backed down without a fight, King's policy proved correct. This was the beginning of the end of Canada always agreeing to British requests.

In 1923, Canada and the United States came to an agreement about fishing for halibut. King insisted that Canada, not Great Britain, sign the treaty. That evening, he dined with the **governor general**. King told the governor general that he was sure it was right for Canada to be independent of Great Britain.

During the 1923 and 1926 conferences between Great Britain and its colonies, King pushed for each colony to have control over its dealings with other countries. Similar to a family, King explained, the colonies were like children. They would grow up and be on good terms with their mother only if they were given freedom to make their own decisions.

In 1926, Britain gave equal status to all the members of the British Commonwealth of Nations. A Commonwealth flag was designed that consisted of the Commonwealth symbol in gold on a blue background. The "C" represented the word Commonwealth, and the radiating spears represented the many ways that members cooperated. The word "British" was dropped from the British Commonwealth of Nations in 1946.

The equal status gave Canada the freedom to make its own decisions. As a result, Canada established **legations** in the United States in 1926, France in 1928, and Japan in 1929.

The Imperial Conference of 1923, which included British politician Lord Curzon, British Prime Minister Stanley Baldwin, Canadian diplomat Vincent Massey, King, and Australian Prime Minister Stanley Bruce, set in motion the independence of Canada from Great Britain.

Women in Parliament

The 1921 election was the first time women were allowed to vote in federal elections. It was also the first time women were allowed to be members of Parliament. Of the five women who ran as candidates, only Agnes Macphail won. Macphail, a school teacher in rural Ontario, defeated 10 men to win the nomination. She then spent two months convincing the voters that her gender would not prevent her from looking after their interests. In the House of Commons, she felt very isolated and lonely. As the only woman in Parliament, Macphail faced considerable pressure. The press paid more attention to what she wore than to what she said. "I was intensely unhappy," she recalled.

Macphail was very serious about her job and rejected several marriage proposals to remain in Ottawa. She fought for equality for women, peaceful solutions to international conflicts, family allowances, old age and disability pensions, and better conditions for workers and prisoners. Macphail was re-elected four times, but it was not until 1935 that another woman member of Parliament was elected.

Now that women had the vote and could be elected to the House of Commons, they wanted the opportunity to be senators. Since the prime minister appoints senators, several women's groups petitioned Prime Minister Robert Borden in 1919 to appoint a woman senator. During the next eight years, Prime Ministers Arthur

> **"I couldn't open my mouth to say the simplest thing without it appearing in the papers. I was a curiosity, a freak. And you know the way the world treats freaks."**
>
> *Agnes Macphail on being the first woman in the House of Commons*

Meighen and King ignored similar requests. They argued that the Constitution of Canada said that only "persons" could be appointed and that women did not qualify as "persons."

Emily Murphy, Nellie McClung, Louise McKinney, Henrietta Muir Edwards, and Irene Parlby joined together to challenge the definition of "persons" in the Constitution. These prominent women from Alberta became known as "the Famous Five." All five women were married, had children, and were active in politics.

In 1928, the **Supreme Court of Canada** ruled that "persons" did not include women. The Famous Five took their case to Great Britain. The following year, the British court reversed this decision. In 1930, King appointed Cairine Wilson to the **Senate** as Canada's first woman senator.

Although Agnes Macphail was thought of primarily as a feminist, she also spent a great deal of time addressing tariff issues in Parliament.

The "King-Byng Wing Ding"

By 1925, the economy was doing well, and King decided to call an election. The Liberals only won 99 seats. The Conservatives captured 116 seats. The Progressives took 24 seats. No party held a majority of seats.

Many people, including Governor General Julian Byng, thought that King would resign and allow Arthur Meighen to become prime minister. King refused to resign. He hoped that the Progressive Party would support him. This would give him a majority in the **House of Commons**. He passed an old-age pensions law to get their support.

A government scandal ruined King's plans. Civil servants in King's administration were caught smuggling goods into Canada from the United States. Meighen tried to win the support of the Progressive Party to vote King out of power.

Before this could happen, King asked Governor General Byng to call another election. When Byng refused, Meighen became prime minister. King wrote in his diary "If Meighen seeks to carry on I believe he will not go far. Our chances of winning out in a general election are good."

King was correct. The Progressive Party did not support Meighen for very long. This time, Governor General Byng agreed when Meighen asked him to call an election.

In the campaign for the 1926 election, King argued that Byng had been wrong to refuse the prime minister's request for an election. King posed as the champion of Canadian independence against the British-appointed governor general. This constitutional issue distracted voters from the "**customs scandal.**" The Liberals won 116 seats. With the support of the Progressives, King became prime minister for the second time.

The King and Byng confrontation is known in Canadian politics as the "King-Byng Wing Ding."

Following his term as governor general, Byng returned to Great Britain. He became Viscount Byng of Vimy in 1926.

GOVERNOR GENERAL LORD JULIAN BYNG

Lord Byng was governor general of Canada from 1921 to 1926. He commanded Canadian troops in World War I. In 1921, for the first time, Great Britain asked the Canadian government who it would like as governor general. Prime Minister Arthur Meighen preferred a non-military person, but Byng was chosen because he was willing and available.

King and Dictators

When King returned to power in 1935, the world situation was very tense. Italian dictator Benito Mussolini was looking to conquer land in Africa. German Adolf Hitler was preparing to conquer Europe, and in Russia, communist leader Joseph Stalin hated western democracies.

King wanted to avoid a war. He knew that if Great Britain declared war against Germany, Canada would also be drawn into the war. This would probably lead to conscription, which would divide French- and English-speaking Canada. At the Imperial Conference of 1937, King urged Great Britain to agree to Hitler's demands rather than go to war.

> "So far as war is concerned, you need have no fear of war at the instance of Germany. We have no desire for war; our people don't want war, and we don't want war."
>
> *Hitler to King; excerpt from King's diary, June 29, 1937*

When British Prime Minister Neville Chamberlain agreed to let Hitler take control of part of Czechoslovakia, King sent Chamberlain a telegram of appreciation. "What a happy man Chamberlain must be, and what an example he has set to the world in perseverance of a just cause," King wrote.

On one occasion, King spoke with Hitler for more than an hour. He showed Hitler the biography of himself and pointed out a picture of the cottage where he was born in Berlin, Ontario. King praised the good work of Hitler's regime. King wrote in his diary, "As I talked with him, I could not but think of Joan of Arc. He is distinctly a mystic... He is a teetotaler and also a vegetarian; is unmarried, [moderate] in all his habits and ways."

At the end of their meeting, Hitler gave King an autographed photograph of himself. King wrote, "My sizing up of the man as I sat and talked with him was that he is really one who truly loves his fellow men, and his country, and would make any sacrifice

King was fond of Hitler when the two first met in 1937. His opinion changed dramatically after World War II.

for their good." Hitler appeared to be "a man of deep sincerity and a genuine patriot." Once the war began, King's opinion of Hitler changed radically.

At the end of World War II, King went to Nuremberg, Germany, where some of the German military leaders were tried for war crimes. He watched some of the proceedings from the front row of the gallery. He blamed Hitler for the war. "It really was a horrible and pathetic, tragic sight to see the men and to think that that particular group of men under one leader—a maniac, a devil incarnate—had been able to bring destruction upon themselves, their country and the world to the extent they have and, worst of all, destruction to moral standards."

KING VISITS HITLER

King had been a very successful labour negotiator. He believed that he could use this talent to prevent another world war. King was in Great Britain for the coronation of George VI, and decided to visit Germany. King arrived in Berlin, Germany, in June 1937. He hoped to convince Hitler not to go to war. During his first two days in Germany, King visited the **Hitler youth camps**, the **Jewish labour camps**, and the Olympic stadium.

King attended the Nuremberg Trials in the Palace of Justice, in the city of Nuremberg. The trials began in November 1945 and lasted for 218 days.

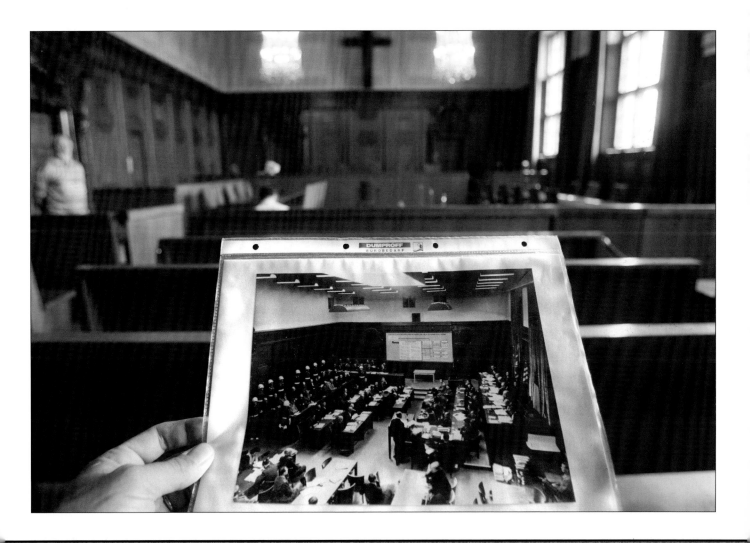

King and World War II

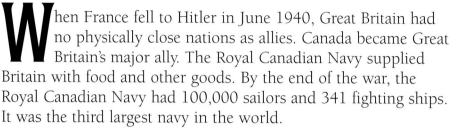

"How just the retribution that has overtaken the followers of Hitler and Mussolini. It is sad beyond words that the innocent have had to suffer so terribly."

King's diary excerpt on Germany's surrender during World War II

When France fell to Hitler in June 1940, Great Britain had no physically close nations as allies. Canada became Great Britain's major ally. The Royal Canadian Navy supplied Britain with food and other goods. By the end of the war, the Royal Canadian Navy had 100,000 sailors and 341 fighting ships. It was the third largest navy in the world.

Canadian pilots helped stop Germany from winning the Battle of Britain and other air battles. Most of the Commonwealth pilots were trained in Canada. Canadian soldiers fought on the battlefields of Europe and Asia. They played an important role in Italy and in the final invasion of Western Europe after D-Day.

At home, Canadians produced supplies for the war. By the end of World War II, one in ten Canadians worked in war plants. They produced 900,000 rifles, 800,000 military vehicles, 244,000 machine guns, 16,000 airplanes, and 6,500 tanks. Women worked in the factories and joined the armed forces. The war helped Canada become a modern industrialized nation.

In 1942, all Canadians received a ration book. When they bought sugar, butter, meat, tea or coffee, they had to use coupons from their book. When their coupons were used, they could not buy any rationed items legally. Some tried buying goods from the **black market**. If they were caught, they had to pay stiff fines.

Women contributed heavily to the war effort by working in factories making supplies, such as bombs and bullets.

During World War II, Canada produced nearly 6,500 tanks.

Gas was also rationed. Canadians could fill up once a month. They could not buy a new car because car production stopped in 1942. Instead, car plants concentrated on making military vehicles.

Anything Canadians could spare went to the war effort. Butter and cheese that was not purchased by Canadians was sent to Great Britain, where rationing was much more severe. Steel that, at one time, would have been used to make washing machines, now made bombers. Nickels, or 5-cent pieces, were made of copper and zinc because the metal nickel was needed for armour coating on tanks.

The government encouraged Canadians to conserve for the war effort. Families saved metals, rags, papers, rubber, and glass. Bacon fat and bones were saved for making explosives for the war effort. Local clubs canvassed house to house to collect donations. Clothing regulations were brought in to save material. Pant cuffs, ruffles, and double-breasted jackets were no longer produced or sold. Pajamas and housecoats stopped at the ankle to save material.

TIMETABLE FOR WAR

1931
Japan invades Manchuria in northern China.

1933
Hitler comes to power in Germany.

1935
Italy invades Ethiopia.

1936
The Spanish Civil War begins.
Hitler sends German troops into the Rhineland on the French border.
Japan, Italy, and Germany sign treaty of mutual protection.

1937
Japan invades China.

1938
Germany takes over Austria and Czechoslovakia.

1939
Germany invades Poland.
Soviet Union invades Poland and Finland.
Great Britain and France declare war on Germany.
Canada declares war on Germany.

French-Canadians and Conscription

> ### "Not necessarily conscription, but conscription if necessary."
> *King on the issue of conscription*

National unity was King's most important goal. When Great Britain declared war on Germany, King wanted to show French-Canadians that Canada was independent. He said that "Parliament would decide" whether to declare war. Canada entered the war one week later.

King remembered how conscription divided French-speaking and English-speaking Canadians in World War I. He promised that he would not invoke conscription. In June 1940, however, Canada conscripted soldiers.

In 1941, recruitment was slowing down. The next year, King decided to hold a **plebiscite** on the issue of conscription. He asked Canadians if they would release him from his earlier promises not to impose conscription for overseas service. King said that even if the "yes" votes won, there might not be conscription.

In Quebec, 73 percent of people voted "no" to conscription The other provinces voted 80 percent in favour. The country was divided. For the next two years, King tried to avoid the issue. He began a media campaign to recruit volunteers for overseas service. As long as the Canadian Army stayed in Great Britain, there was no need for conscription. Two years later, after the invasion of France, the situation changed. The battle for control of Europe had begun, and the losses of human life were high. The Canadian government tried to recruit men voluntarily. Only a few enlisted.

In 1944, King felt that he had to pass conscription. He ordered 16,000 conscripts overseas, but only 2,463 of them actually saw battle.

Many French-Canadians came to respect King for holding a national referendum on the issue of conscription.

Sergeant Jane Shaddock and Private Polly Pollyblank were members of the first contingent of Canadian Women's Army Corps in Hamm, Germany, in 1945.

Many French-Canadians were angry. However, since King had tried to avoid conscription, the country was not torn apart. One Quebec **cabinet minister** resigned, but most other French-Canadians leaders supported King. Louis St. Laurent, King's "Quebec lieutenant," told Quebeckers that the decision was necessary. Historian Michael Bliss wrote that one of King's major achievements was in "dividing Canadians least."

WOMEN IN THE WAR

By 1941, the armed forces were in desperate need of recruits. Women finally were allowed to enlist. One young woman walked 30 kilometres to a recruiting station. Eventually, Canada had 45,000 service women. They served in a wide variety of non-combat roles, such as radar operators, truck and ambulance drivers, nurses, secretaries, and mechanics. Some women often found themselves in the heat of battle. They were bombed, shelled, and torpedoed. Some were made prisoners of war. Two hundred and forty-four women won medals for bravery.

King and War-Time Pressures

> "The government is of the view that, having regard to the strong feeling that has been aroused against the Japanese during the war and to the extreme difficulty of assimilating Japanese persons in Canada, no immigration of Japanese into this country should be allowed after the war."
>
> *King's speech, House of Commons, August 1944*

Throughout the 1930s and 1940s, King faced a number of challenges, including pressure from Canadian society to limit the rights of cultural groups living in Canada and to allow fewer people to immigrate to Canada.

During World War II, many people believed Canada should be kept safe from people who were considered dangerous. The presence of Communists, Germans, Italians, and Japanese people living in Canada concerned the government. In response, the government banned the Communist Party from practising in Canada, and Germans, Italians, and Japanese people were forced to live in internment camps. Many German Canadians were sent to southern Alberta, where they were forced to work as farm labourers. About 700 Italian Canadians were sent to internment camps.

The S.S. *St. Louis* docked in Antwerp, Belgium, with hundreds of German-Jewish refugees, before the ship was denied admittance to Cuba, the United States, and Canada.

In December 1941, the Japanese attacked the American naval base at Pearl Harbor, in Hawaii. They then attacked Hong Kong, Indonesia, and Malaysia, and swept through the islands of the Pacific. Many Canadians feared that British Columbia might be the next target. This fear turned to panic when a Japanese submarine was seen off the coast of Vancouver Island in 1942. King ordered that all people in Canada of Japanese descent be moved away from the coastal regions of British Columbia. They were sent to isolated camps in places such as Kelowna, British Columbia, and Lethbridge, Alberta. Some men were sent as labourers to farms on the Prairies and in Ontario. About 24,000 Japanese Canadians were relocated. Families were separated. Men were sent to one camp, women and children to another. In addition, Japanese language schools and newspapers were closed, and more than 1,200 fishing boats owned by Japanese Canadians were seized.

King's government interned many Japanese-Canadians during World War II.

King's Diaries

> "After being told by many that I could never keep a diary, I decided to make at least an attempt. Accordingly I secured this book about 4 P.M. this afternoon. "
>
> *King's diary excerpt*

King was a champion diary writer. He wrote his first diary words in 1893 when he was 18 years old. When he dictated his final entry in 1950, he was 75 years old. His diaries are approximately 30,000 pages long. A stack of paper this size would reach the rim of a basketball net.

When King began his first diary in 1893, he declared that he had several objectives. Writing the journal each day would be good self-discipline. The diary would enable "the reader... to trace how the author has sought to improve his time." He also hoped that his friends would "find great pleasure... in the remembrance of events recorded." King promised to make the diary a true account of his life.

Soon, the diary became a friend with whom he could share his secret thoughts and feelings. He also used the diary to give himself advice. He complained about gaining weight or wasting time at parties. He promised the diary that he would do better and work harder.

King's will ordered that his diary be destroyed, "except the parts which I have indicated." However, he never indicated what parts he wanted saved. As a result, all of his diary entries are now available to be read.

King's diaries were approximately 30,000 pages long. If they were stacked on top of one another, they would reach more than 3 metres tall.

King and the United States

One of the most important results of World War II was the new partnership between Canada and the United States. Prime Minister King and President Franklin Roosevelt were on close personal terms. An invitation to King from Roosevelt led to the Ogdensburg Agreement. This agreement created a joint system of defence.

Another result of King and Roosevelt's partnership was the Hyde Park Agreement in 1941. It resulted from a telephone call from King to Roosevelt. This agreement tied Canada more closely to the American economy and brought greater prosperity.

Shortly after the United States entered the war, work began on the construction of the Alaska Highway. In 1942 and 1943, American soldiers and Canadian and American civilians built an all-weather, gravel road that stretched 2,451 kilometres from Dawson Creek, British Columbia, to Fairbanks, Alaska. The workers battled extremes of hot, cold, wet, and dry weather. Miraculously, the road was completed. One stretch, known as "Suicide Hill," bore a sign that warned people to "Prepare to Meet Thy God." The highway is a tribute to Canadian and American perseverance and organizational skills.

The close friendship of King with U.S. President Roosevelt as well as British Prime Minister Winston Churchill helped win the war. In the early years of the war, King often acted as a go-between for the United States and Britain.

King signed the United Nations Charter in San Francisco in 1945. Article I sets forth the principal concerns of the United Nations: international peace and security; friendly relations among nations; international co-operation in solving international problems of an economic, social, cultural, or humanitarian character.

> **"Both of us enjoyed so completely the afternoon drive, the talk together, and the delightful conversation at the dinner table and felt we were sharing so completely the different matters discussed, the enjoyment of Hyde Park, and his own ideals, etc. that he really was in the happiest and freest possible moods."**
>
> *King's diary excerpt about his day with Roosevelt after signing the Hyde Park Agreement, April 20, 1941*

King's Final Years

> "I felt I had [political] power by being true to the people and to the promises I had given them. I did not think it was a mark of leadership to try to make the people do what one wanted them to do."
>
> *King's diary excerpt reflecting on his career, 1940*

King was not a dynamic figure. In 1946, only 8 out of 100 Canadians picked King as the living person they most admired. Yet, he was prime minister longer than any other Canadian. He held office for almost 22 years—from 1921 to 1930, and from 1935 to 1948. The second-longest-serving prime minister was John A. Macdonald, who spent almost 19 years in office.

Upon King's death, tributes to his long and successful career came from a variety of world leaders. Several provincial premiers called King a great nation builder. The **premier** of New Brunswick, John B. Macnair, said that King was the greatest Canadian of his generation. King is pictured on the 50-dollar bill.

Louis St. Laurent became prime minister when King retired in 1948 and held the position for almost eight years after King's death in 1950.

As a young man, King had been interested in helping the less fortunate. In 1926, he created old-age pensions. These provided financial support for senior citizens. In 1940, King's unemployment insurance act helped people financially while they looked for jobs. Five years later, family allowances helped parents support their children.

In 1937, King set up a Royal Commission on Dominion-Provincial Relations. This Rowell-Sirois Commission supported important changes in the tax system. These changes helped federal provincial cooperation. The commission suggested giving more federal money to the less wealthy provinces than to the wealthier provinces.

Prior to 1947, Canadians were considered British subjects living in Canada. Canada was the first Commonwealth country to create its own citizenship. "I speak as a citizen of Canada," said King in 1947. At the first Canadian citizenship ceremony, King was given the first Canadian citizenship certificate. His number was 0001.

The burden of politics affected King's health. He resigned as party leader in August 1948, and as prime minister on November 15. After his retirement, he wrote in his diary that he was a tired and lonely man. His health began to fail. He became too exhausted to write his **memoirs**. William Lyon Mackenzie King died on July 22, 1950. He was buried in the family plot at Mount Pleasant Cemetery in Toronto.

King was one of Canada's most important nation builders.

"His tenure as prime minister of Canada, exceeding 21 years, was distinguished as it was extended. He brought his country to a new stature of greatness. His passing marks the close of an epoch in the life of our neighbour to the north."
U.S. President Harry Truman on King's death

Arthur Meighen

Throughout his political career, Meighen was known as an accomplished debater.

Arthur Meighen was Canada's ninth prime minister. His ability to recall facts and figures amazed people. Arthur Meighen was one of the best political debaters and speakers in Canadian history. However, this was not enough to keep him in power. Twice, Meighen was elected prime minister. Both times he lost the following election.

Arthur Meighen was born in 1874 in Anderson, Ontario. He studied mathematics, and later law, at the University of Toronto. After graduating, Meighen became a teacher and a salesman. In 1903, he opened a law practice in Portage la Prairie, Manitoba.

In 1908, Meighen was elected to the House of Commons. He achieved a national reputation in 1913, when he helped find a way to allow the government to end a debate on a bill. Meighen's debating skills brought him to the attention of Conservative Party leader Robert Borden. When Borden became prime minister in 1911, he asked Meighen to decide how to pass conscription and to **nationalize** the railways to create the Canadian National Railway.

As a result of his abilities and his hard work during World War I, Meighen became prime minister when Borden resigned on July 10, 1920.

In the election the following year, voters were not happy with the Conservative government for mistakes made during World War I. French-Canadians disliked Meighen because he favoured conscription. King won the election. Meighen had been prime minister for less than five months.

Over the next four years, Meighen worked hard to rebuild the Conservative Party. In the 1925 election, the Conservatives won the most seats. However, King kept power by forming an alliance with the Progressive Party.

In June 1926, it appeared that King would lose the support of the Progressive Party. He asked Governor General Lord Byng to call another election. When Byng refused to do so, King resigned. Instead of calling another election, Byng asked Meighen to become prime minister. Less than three months later, Meighen asked the governor general to call an election. King won the 1926 election. Meighen resigned as Conservative Party leader soon after.

Meighen's Missing Overcoat

Meighen could remember long quotes from famous authors, but he would sometimes forget to carry an umbrella, wear shoes, and attend dinner invitations. He once arrived in the House of Commons wearing his bedroom slippers. He was not interested in fashion. Meighen wore an old green overcoat for so many years that it became very worn. His colleagues became so tired of the coat that they threw it away. A railway worker found the coat, saw Meighen's name in it, and returned the coat. Meighen did not know that it had been missing. He wore it for several more years, to the dismay of his colleagues.

Richard Bedford Bennett

Richard Bedford Bennett was prime minister during the Great Depression of the 1930s—one of Canada's most difficult eras.

Richard Bedford Bennett was born in Hopewell, New Brunswick, in 1870. His father tried shipbuilding and farming, but never made much money. Bennett's childhood fostered a lifelong habit of thrift. His mother was the driving force in the family. She taught her son to work as hard as he could, save money, and give to charity.

Bennett was smart. Hard work and little play was his motto. He was a good student. By age 18, he was the principal of four schools. At age 20, Bennett stated that he would some day be the prime minister. Bennett saved enough money to study law at Dalhousie University. He graduated in 1893.

In 1897, he moved to Calgary and became a junior partner in Senator James A. Lougheed's law offices. Lougheed, like Bennett's parents, was a Conservative. Lougheed, who was the richest man in Calgary, once said that "Bennett can solve any problem he puts his mind to... some day Bennett will be called upon to solve the greatest problems in Canada."

In 1911, Bennett was elected to the House of Commons. He later became leader of the Conservative Party. In 1930, Bennett's Conservative Party won the federal election, and he became prime minister. He soon had to deal with the Great Depression. The voters blamed the lack of jobs on Bennett, and in the 1935 election, King defeated him. Bennett remained the Conservative leader until 1938. He moved to Great Britain, where he was made **viscount** in 1941 and sat in the House of Lords. He died in 1947.

"I am not interested in politics. I am here in Ottawa as prime minister today and I may be gone tomorrow. I don't care. Life has given me about everything a man can desire... if I can do anything for Canada, that is what I want to do."
Bennett, 1931

Bennett's Ambitions

Bennett's three ambitions were to become a millionaire, prime minister, and a peer in the British Empire. He achieved his first ambition thanks to his wealthy clients. They included the Canadian Pacific Railway and Calgary Power. He also inherited a great deal of money from a friend. He became prime minister in 1930 and a viscount in Great Britain in 1941.

Bennett and the Great Depression

The U.S. **stock market** crashed in 1929. The Great Depression had begun. Unemployment and hard economic times spread around the world. Countries that bought Canadian wheat, fish, wood, and other goods could no longer afford them. Eighty percent of the products made by Canadian farms, forests, and mines were sold abroad. To help their own people, many countries put a **tariff** on Canadian imports. The United States taxed Canadian cattle and dairy products. When Spain, Portugal, and Italy taxed Canadian dried cod and fresh fish, it crippled the Atlantic fishing industry.

Canada's manufacturing fared no better. Many Canadian businesses had too many goods to sell. Few could afford to buy cars, shoes, radios, dresses, or appliances. Factories and businesses closed down or laid off workers. Many

businesses and individuals could not repay their loans. They went **bankrupt**. The people who supplied the raw materials to make these products lost their jobs. People could no longer afford to pay for furniture, cars, and even their homes.

By 1933, one in five Canadian workers was unemployed. There was no employment insurance. Two million Canadians relied upon a government relief program to sustain them.

The worst place to live during the Depression was on the Prairies. In 1929, wheat sold for $1.60 a **bushel**. By 1932, farmers could barely sell their crop for $0.38 a bushel. The weather brought more trouble. The summer of 1931 was a particularly dry year. **Drought** returned in 1933. It would be another five years before prairie farmers would see rain again.

Employers fired young, single men first. They assumed that older, married employees supported families and were therefore more dependent on the work. Canada's young men set off to look for work in cities across the country. There were no jobs anyplace. These **drifters** were desperate for food, for shelter, and for work.

Bennett promised to take "whatever action is necessary" to end unemployment. He immediately provided $20 million for the unemployed. To protect Canadian jobs, Bennett placed high taxes on imported goods, which made Canadian goods cheaper to purchase than

During the Depression, young men often drifted from town to town looking for work by jumping onto and riding freight trains.

foreign goods. Bennett also tried to promote more trade within the British Commonwealth. These were positive measures, but the lines outside the **soup kitchens** only grew longer.

Just before the 1935 election, Bennett proposed a series of government-enforced working conditions, including an eight-hour workday, a minimum wage, grants to farmers, health and unemployment insurance, and price controls. "The old order is gone," he told a surprised radio audience. However, voters wanted to know why it had taken five years for the government to take action. King and the Liberal Party told voters that they had to choose between "King or Chaos." They chose King.

Bennett could not end the Great Depression. He was, however, successful in creating a few lasting agencies. In 1932, he created the Canadian Radio Broadcasting Commission, which was the forerunner of the Canadian Broadcasting Corporation, and in 1935, he developed the Bank of Canada and the Canadian Wheat Board.

> "I propose that any government of which I am the head will... initiate whatever action is necessary to that end, or perish in the attempt."
>
> *Bennett on dealing with unemployment, June 9, 1930*

The Canadian Radio Broadcasting Commission, forerunner to the CBC, was one of R.B. Bennett's accomplishments as prime minister.

Timeline

1870s	1880s	1890s	1900s

PRIME MINISTERS

King is born in Berlin, Ontario on December 17, 1874.	John A. Macdonald is prime minister for the entire decade and remains in office until 1891.	King graduates from the University of Toronto in 1895.	King is elected to the House of Commons on October 26, 1908.

CANADA

Manitoba becomes a province in 1870. British Columbia enters Confederation in 1871. Prince Edward Island joins Confederation in 1873.	The first kindergarten opens in Toronto in 1883. Calixa Lavallee writes Canada's national anthem in 1880. NATIONAL ANTHEM / HYMNE NATIONAL O CANADA	James Naismith invents basketball in 1891. Labour Day is celebrated for the first time on September 3, 1894.	Alberta and Saskatchewan become provinces in 1905. L. M. Montgomery publishes *Anne of Green Gables* in 1908.

WORLD

Jules Verne publishes, *Around the World in 80 Days,* and Louisa May Alcott writes *Little Women* in 1871. The National Baseball League is created in 1874.	Karl Marx dies in 1883. Thomas Edison invents the light bulb in 1880.	Thomas Edison invents the motion picture in 1891.	The Wright brothers fly the first airplane in 1900. Queen Victoria dies in 1901.

1910s   1920s   1930s

PRIME MINISTERS

King's mother dies on December 18, 1917.

King is elected leader of the Liberal Party on August 7, 1919.

King becomes prime minister on December 21, 1921.

King gets his dog, Pat, in 1924.

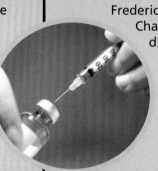

King meets with Hitler in May 1937.

Canada declares war on Germany on September 10, 1939.

CANADA

The Winnipeg General Strike takes place from May 15 to June 26, 1919.

Frederick Banting and Charles Best discover insulin in 1921.

Cairine Wilson becomes the first female senator in 1930.

The Canadian Broadcasting Corporation (CBC) is created in 1936.

WORLD

World War I takes place from 1914–1918.

The first Technicolor full-length film in premiers in 1992.

Television is invented in 1929.

Germany attacks Poland on September 1, 1939.

Great Britain declares war on Germany on September 3, 1939.

Did You Know?

King's grandfather, William Lyon Mackenzie, was the first mayor of Toronto.

King and Bennett are the only two prime ministers to never marry.

On King's 25th anniversary of becoming leader of the Liberal Party, he was given a statuette of himself and his dog, Pat.

During the Great Depression, car owners could not afford to buy gasoline. They often harnessed a team of horses or oxen to pull their cars. These horse-pulled cars became known as "Bennett Buggies."

In 1990, one of Meighen's grandsons, Michael Meighen, was appointed to the Canadian Senate.

Bennett is the only deceased prime minister who is not buried in Canada.

The last ship launched at Bennett's father's shipyard was the *Sir John A. Macdonald*.

Test Your Knowledge

Multiple:

Where was Arthur Meighen born?

A) Anderson, Ontario
B) London, England
C) Toronto, Ontario

A) Anderson, Ontario

Multiple:

Who was the first woman appointed to the Senate?

A) Joan Patteson
B) Cairine Wilson
C) Nellie McClung

B) Cairine Wilson

Question:

In what year were the Japanese interned during World War II?

1942

Question:

Who was Canada's longest-serving prime minister?

King

Multiple:

What political party did Arthur Meighen belong to?

A) Conservative Party
B) Liberal Party
C) Progressive Party

A) Conservative Party

Question:

What was the name of King's dog?

Pat

Question:

Which prime minister talked to the dead?

King

Question:

Which prime minister was a millionaire?

Bennett

Question:

Which prime minister introduced old age pensions?

King

Activity

The Great Depression was the longest economic collapse in the history of the industrialized world. The beginning was marked by the U.S. stock market crash in 1929, known as "Black Monday." Businesses and banks closed their doors, and people lost their jobs, homes, and savings. One in five Canadians was unemployed and unable to provide for their families. Young men drifted from town to town looking for work.

To understand what life was like for people during the Great Depression, visit the library, and look up newspaper articles written and printed during the 1930s. Many libraries have online databases of archived newspapers as well as microfilm. Most newspapers keep a copy of all of their old editions. Try arranging a visit to a local newspaper office that was in operation during the 1930s.

After researching and reading several news items from the Great Depression, choose a particular event and day from the 1930s, and write your own article about it. You can use information from other news articles, but write down the events in your own words.

Try to find a photo that goes with your story from the library or online. Copy the image with a scanner or photocopier at school and glue it onto your article. Remember to write an eye-catching, exciting title.

Further Research

Books

To find out more about Canadian prime ministers, visit your local library. Most libraries have computers that connect to a database for researching information. If you input a key word, you will be provided with a list of books in the library that contain information on that topic. Non-fiction books are arranged numerically, using their call number. Fiction books are organized alphabetically by the author's last name.

Websites

The World Wide Web is also a good source of information. Reputable websites usually include government sites, educational sites, and online encyclopedias. Visit the following sites to learn more about Canadian prime ministers.

Read the diary of William Lyon Mackenzie King at Library and Archives of Canada's website.
www.collectionscanada.ca/king

Enter "King: Public Life, Private Man" into the search engine on CBC's Digital Archives website, and watch digital documentaries about King.
www.cbc.ca/archives

Visit Collections Canada, and click on "speeches" at the bottom of the screen to read some of King's and Bennett's speeches.
www.collectionscanada.ca/primeministers/index-e.html

Glossary

bankrupt: unable to pay back debts

black market: a place where illegal goods or goods at illegal prices or quantities are sold

bushel: a unit for measuring the volume of grain, fruits, vegetables, and other dry foods

colony: a region ruled by a country that is usually far away

conscription: the compulsory enlistment of people in the armed forces

customs: the department of the government that collects a duty on imported goods

drifters: people who move from place to place or job to job

drought: a long period of dry weather

Great Depression: the longest and worst period of high unemployment and low sales of products during the 1930s

Hitler youth camps: places where young people were trained by a military organization of the Nazi Party to become future soldiers

Jewish labour camps: places where Jewish people were forced to live and work during World War II

labour unions: organized groups of workers who campaign for the rights of their members

medium: a person through whom spirits of the dead can supposedly communicate with the living

memoirs: accounts of someone's life written by them

rebellion: a revolt against the government that is in power

séances: meetings at which people believe they can contact the dead

soup kitchens: places that provide free food to the less fortunate; soup kitchens were especially common during the Great Depression

spirit: a ghost

stock market: a place where stocks and bonds are bought and sold

tariff: tax on imported and exported goods

unemployment: the state of being without a job

viscount: a nobleman ranking below an earl or a count

Political Terms

cabinet minister: an elected member of Parliament chosen by the prime minister to be responsible for a specific area, for example, health or aboriginal affairs

civil service: people who work for the administration of the government

Confederation: the event in 1867 when Canada became its own country; the original four provinces were Quebec, Ontario, Nova Scotia, and New Brunswick

governor general: the representative of the British monarch in Canada

House of Commons: people who have been elected from across Canada to make laws for the whole country

legations: offices overseas that represent another country

nationalize: to bring an industry under the control or ownership of a nation

Parliament: the House of Commons and the Senate

plebiscite: a direct vote by voters of a country, province, or municipality on a question

premier: a Canadian province's head of government

Senate: a group of people made up of representatives from each province who review laws passed by the House of Commons

Supreme Court of Canada: the highest court in Canada

Upper Canada: mostly English-speaking colony created by Great Britain in 1791, re-named Canada West in 1841 when it united with Lower Canada (Canada East) to form the United Province of Canada. Today, Upper Canada is known as Ontario.

Index

Bennett, Richard 5, 13, 36, 37, 38, 39, 42, 43, 45
Berlin, Ontario 8, 12, 22, 40
Byng, Julian 21, 35

Commonwealth 7, 18, 19, 24, 33, 39
conscription 12, 22, 26, 27, 35, 46
Conservative Party 12, 13, 18, 35, 43

debating 8, 35
diary 7, 8, 11, 14, 15, 16, 21

election 9, 12, 13, 16, 20, 21

Famous Five 20

governor general 18, 21, 35, 47
Great Britain 6, 18, 19, 20, 21, 22, 23, 24, 25, 26, 37, 41, 47
Great Depression 7, 12, 13, 36, 37, 38, 39, 42, 44, 46

Hitler, Adolf 22, 23, 24, 25, 41, 46
House of Commons 20, 21, 28, 35, 37, 40, 47

internment camps 28

Laurier, Wilfrid 4, 12, 16
Liberal Party 9, 12, 39, 41, 42, 43

King, William Lyon Mackenzie 5, 6, 7, 8, 9, 10, 11, 12, 13, 14, 15, 16, 17, 18, 19, 20, 21, 22, 23, 24, 26, 27, 28, 29, 30, 31, 32, 33, 35, 37, 39, 40, 41, 42, 43

Macphail, Agnes 20
Meighen, Arthur 5, 12, 18, 20, 21, 34, 35, 42, 43

Parliament 9, 12, 18, 20, 26, 47
Pat 14, 15, 41, 42, 43

Senate 20, 42, 43, 47
St. Laurent, Louis 12, 13, 27, 32

United States 8, 9, 18, 19, 21, 28, 31, 38

women's rights 20
World War II 7, 22, 23, 24, 25, 28, 29, 31, 43, 46
Wriedt, Etta 16